THEY'RE PLAYING YOUR SONG, CHARLIE BROWN

by CHARLES M. SCHULZ

Selected cartoons from
WIN A FEW, LOSE A FEW, CHARLIE BROWN, Vol. 2

FAWCETT CREST · NEW YORK

THEY'RE PLAYING YOUR SONG, CHARLIE BROWN

This book, prepared especially for Fawcett Crest Books, a unit of
CBS Publications, the Consumer Publishing Division of CBS Inc.,
comprises the second half of WIN A FEW, LOSE A FEW,
CHARLIE BROWN and is reprinted by arrangement with Holt,
Rinehart and Winston, Inc.

ISBN: 0-449-23364-2

Printed in the United States of America

11   10   9   8   7   6   5   4

THEY'RE PLAYING
YOUR SONG,
CHARLIE BROWN

Dear Santa Claus,
Do not bring me any presents this year.
I want my Christmas to be one of peace and love, not greed.
Getting a lot of presents is for the birds
!
THAT'S ONLY AN EXPRESSION!!
SCHULZ

Winter had come again all too soon, and it was time for Joe Jacket to bring in his polar cows.

As he rode out from the barn, the first flakes of snow began to fall.

He looked up at the slate-gray sky and shivered.
The blizzard started quickly. A howling wind pounded the snow across the bleak prairie.
Joe Jacket hunched forward in the saddle, and urged his mount forward through the flying snow and screaming wind.
TELL MY PUBLISHERS NOT TO EXPECT A MANUSCRIPT UNTIL SPRING!
SCHULZ

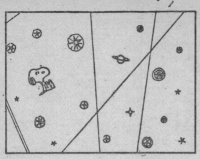

Dear Grandma,
I had a very nice birthday.
Thank you for the doll. It is very real.
In fact, it is a little too real.
When I go some place, I have to hire a sitter!
SCHULZ